Song of Solomon

A Descriptive Word for Word
Translation of the
Bride and the Bridegroom

by
Scott C. Lovett

Fervent Fire Productions
Tulsa, Oklahoma

Unless otherwise indicated, all Old and New Testament Scripture quotations are taken from the *King James Version, 1769 edition* of the Bible.

The Song of Solomon

ISBN# 9781604589177

Copyright © 2012 by Scott C. Lovett

Fervent Fire Evangelistic Ministries

315 S. Sheridan Road

Tulsa, OK 74112

Published by Fervent Fire Productions

315 S. Sheridan Road

Tulsa, OK 74112

Printed in the United States of America. All rights reserved under International Copyright Law. Contents and/or cover may not be reproduced in whole or in part in any form without the express written consent of the Publisher.

Dedication

I would like to dedicate this work to God and His beautiful Bride, a chaste virgin, a mature and dedicated people of commitment and sincerity of heart, a remnant group of believers who desire to follow His Word and yield to His Spirit until they bear His image in the earth.

...to the multitudes that are deceiving and being deceived, believing the varied opinions of men without finding true doctrine in the Word of God. To a generation of men and women who do what is right in their own eyes, and have failed to submit to the Lordship of Jesus Christ. May you die to self and lay your life down as He did, bearing His image to those you value in your life. Instead of looking for others to embrace personal sin that damages those around you, acknowledge your fault, have love for Jesus, desire to change for Him, receive the freeing truth of the Word, without compromise, expecting the power of God to make you a new and living example that bears His image in the earth.

Contents

Introduction: The Drowing Heart — 5

The Song of Solomon Rules — 29

Chapter 1 — 32

Chapter 2 — 38

Chapter 3 — 44

Chapter 4 — 49

Chapter 5 — 55

Chapter 6 — 61

Chapter 7 — 66

Chapter 8 — 71

The Growing Heart

The expression of love is one of the most misunderstood areas ever sought out within our society. Many think the power of love resides in a rose, others within sweet words simply spoken in a moment, some consider it to be simply fulfilling the carnal desires of another. The descriptive narrative you are about to read is not just a mere representation of the love relationship between a man and a woman. It is much deeper and intimate than the simple act of natural bodily love that seems to be expressed within its pages at first glance. If love were simply the carnal act of human sexuality, then every human being would be able to find complete fulfillment in the carnal act of bodily desire. Yet the multitudes, led by the desire to find fulfillment, seek to find the one true love that will quench their insatiable desire to be complete. Limiting love to a bodily act leads many to multiple partners, dysfunctional marriages, and even perverted forms of sexuality that cause abuse to themselves and others as they search for true fulfillment.

The carnality of mankind has caused multitudes to miss the true fulfillment of love simply by limiting true love as an outward act. As we know, Solomon in all his wisdom failed this test when he searched for true intimacy in the arms of many. His downfall was not failing in kingdom management, but it was in his inability to satisfy the inward. He turned from His inward desire and fed the desire of the outward. Seven hundred wives, and three hundred concubines later, Solomon had destroyed the most intimate love he had sought to obtain, his intimate love for God.

I Kings 11:2-10

"Solomon clave unto these in love. And he had seven hundred wives, princesses, and three hundred concubines: and his wives turned away his heart. For it came to pass, when Solomon was old, *that* his wives turned away his heart after other gods: and his heart was not perfect with the LORD his God, as *was* the heart of David his father. For Solomon went after Ashtoreth the goddess of the Zidonians, and after Milcom the abomination of the Ammonites. And Solomon did evil in the sight of the LORD, and went not fully after the LORD, as *did* David his father. [7]Then did Solomon build an high place for Chemosh, the abomination of Moab, in the hill that *is* before Jerusalem, and for Molech, the abomination of the children of Ammon. And likewise did he for all his strange wives, which burnt incense and sacrificed unto their gods. And the LORD was angry with Solomon, because his heart was turned from the LORD God of Israel, which had appeared unto him twice, And had commanded him concerning this thing, that he should not go after other gods: but he kept not that which the LORD commanded."

Multiple loves will never bring the fulfillment of love, instead the very opposite will take place. Those who endeavor down this path will be destroyed and will never find the fulfillment that they seek. For love is not found in the multitudes, but rather in the singleness of a heart yielded to loving God.

The deep longing of Solomon's heart would not be found in the multitude of things he possessed, or in the arms of the women that filled his court, but the love he sought would be found in the wisdom, which filled his heart in the beginning. When he asked for wisdom he was asking to be filled with God himself, for truth is the absolute of all wisdom and is found in none other than God. In John 14:6, Jesus said, "I am the way, the truth, and the life, no man cometh unto the Father, but by me." When Solomon asked for wisdom above all else, he failed to realize that he was asking for God. The search for truth is the search for God, and those who find wisdom through His Word will grow into a deep love relationship causing their inner man to expand and grow in love.

I Kings 4:29-32

"And God gave Solomon wisdom and understanding exceeding much, and largeness of heart, even as the sand that *is* on the sea shore. [30]And Solomon's wisdom excelled the wisdom of all the children of the east country, and all the wisdom of Egypt. [31]For he was wiser than all men; than Ethan the Ezrahite, and Heman, and Chalcol, and Darda, the sons of Mahol: and his fame was in all nations round about. [32]And he spake three thousand proverbs: and his songs were a thousand and five."

As God filled Solomon with wisdom and understanding his heart grew in size. It grew to the point that he spoke three- thousand proverbs, and sang one- thousand five songs. These moments of intimacy with God were supposed to be the most valuable moments in Solomon's life. As he acquired the wisdom of God he also obtained the blessings of riches and honor, but somewhere along the way his eyes got off of his one true love. They became fixed on the natural loves that surrounded him as the blessing and honor came.

Despite his downfall, God salvaged the greatest of all of Solomon's songs. He preserved the song that revealed the deepest intimacy a people could ever know. Those seeking to fill themselves with the natural act of love have distorted this book and limited it's power to the carnal act of physical intimacy between a man and a woman. In this way, these people remain in the blindness of Solomon and cannot see beyond the natural text. Translators have failed and naturalized one of the most beautiful spiritual texts to ever be written. Within the Hebrew are the hidden, simple, and profound truths of the Bridegroom and His Bride. The apostle Paul understood this when wrote this text in Ephesians.

Ephesians 5:31-33

"For this cause shall a man leave his father and mother, and shall be joined unto his wife, and they two shall be one flesh. ³²This is a great mystery: but I speak concerning Christ and the church. ³³Nevertheless let every one of you in particular so love his wife even as himself; and the wife *see* that she reverence *her* husband."

The Song of Solomon not only reveals who will become the true Bride of Christ, but it unfolds into a dialogue between the Bridegroom, the Bride, and the virgins who say they love Him but fail to measure up. During the progression of this book we find a resounding appeal to the virgins who have failed in their oath to God. We hear the true Bride compelling them to grow in their relationship with the one they say they love. No matter how much intimacy God longs to give us, the carnality of many will keep them from experiencing the spiritual intimacy required to become the Bride. Israel failed this test, yet God pursued them with a veracious passion. He knew that their false lovers would destroy them, so He used his prophets to speak directly to them of the impending danger, and told them what to do to come back underneath His covering of love.

Hosea 3:1

"Then said the LORD unto me, Go yet, love a woman beloved of *her* friend, yet an adulteress, according to the love of the LORD toward the children of Israel, who look to other gods, and love flagons of wine."

There is impending judgment for many who attend church, but fail in the act of inward intimacy and desire for God. To desire God is to obey His wisdom, and to adhere to His Word. You should want to grow in relationship with the Bridegroom, until you literally take on His attributes. Like Solomon, many will be turned away because they loved the blessing more than the intimacy with God. They will fall short in the area of taking on His character and nature, and they will be denied participation in the marriage ceremony. Some virgins want to marry for the wedding gifts, and the provision. The Bride wants to marry to be filled with His love. God is not only a lover, but He is the very love that fills and completes the life of a true Christian. This is what makes us Christ-like. The more you are filled with the intimate desire for His love, the more you become like Him as He fills you with love. Ultimately it will leave you hungry for more until you find complete union with Him, which is being one with Him in both the spiritual and the natural.

The natural virgin divides the spiritual existence and the natural existence, yet God's desire is to bring the natural state of man back to the state of spiritual perfection. The Bible is clear that some will be rejected because they sought after the blessing of the Bridegroom instead of the Bridegroom himself. This is revealed in the seven churches of Revelation, and it is also mentioned in Isaiah.

Isaiah 4:1-4

"And in that day seven women shall take hold of one man, saying, We will eat our own bread, and wear our own apparel: only let us be called by thy name, to take away our reproach.In that day shall the branch of the LORD be beautiful and glorious, and the fruit of the earth *shall be* excellent and comely for them that are escaped of Israel. And it shall come to pass, *that he that is* left in Zion, and *he that* remaineth in Jerusalem, shall be called holy, *even* every one that is written among the living in Jerusalem: When the Lord shall have washed away the filth of the daughters of Zion, and shall have purged the blood of Jerusalem from the midst thereof by the spirit of judgment, and by the spirit of burning."

In this text we see that there are seven women who lay claim to Jesus Christ, but to truly be wed by Him you have to give up your own views of Scripture, and you have to give up your own robes of righteousness. The Bride will love all of Scripture and will deny self-righteousness to obtain His robe of righteousness. The reality for the Christian must be expressed in this. The truth of God is always right, and we are called to believe and desire all of it. We cannot grow into the image of Christ as long as we pick and choose the parts of His Word we are going to eat and be dressed in. Scripture is to be defined by Scripture not the self-righteousness and dogmas of men. We must remember that Satan deceived man by lying to Adam and Eve about partaking of the tree of the knowledge of good and evil. Since that day mankind has been trying to make individual decisions concerning what is good and what is evil. As Christians, we must call the whole Word of God good and have an insatiable desire for its wisdom and experiences.

While many wait for the Bridegrooms return, many virgins

are already failing in the area of true heart commitment. Just because you declare that you are waiting to be wed does not qualify you to be received. The inward flame of the Holy Spirit shows a desire to burn with the passion of Jesus. This passion drives the virgin to obedience in order to be received. It is the Holy Spirit that leads and guides into all truth, and it is the Bridegroom that is the Truth. We know that Jesus alone is the Word made flesh. He is the Bridegroom that we wait and long for. Let's look at the following texts.

John 17:17

"Sanctify them through thy truth: thy word is truth."

I John 5:6

"This is he that came by water and blood, *even* Jesus Christ; not by water only, but by water and blood. And it is the Spirit that beareth witness, because the Spirit is truth."

You see that for the truth of God to burn within us, we must be filled and led by the Holy Spirit. Those who reject any of the truth of God's Word are actually rejecting their opportunity to be united in marriage with Jesus Christ. The work of the Spirit will lead all of us to the same truth and will reveal Jesus in us, through us, and to us. Those virgins in it simply for the benefits fail to fall in love with the Bridegroom simply because they do not love the truth. We find the account of the virgins being separated in Matthew 25:1-11, it says:

"Then shall the kingdom of heaven be likened unto ten virgins, which took their lamps, and went forth to meet the bridegroom. And five of them were wise, and five *were* foolish. They that *were* foolish took their lamps, and took no oil with them: But the wise took oil in their vessels with their lamps. While the bridegroom tarried, they all slumbered and slept. And at midnight there was a cry made, Behold, the bridegroom cometh; go ye out to meet him. Then all those virgins arose, and trimmed their lamps. And the foolish said unto the wise, Give us of your oil; for our lamps are gone out. But the wise answered, saying, *Not so*; lest there be not enough for us and you: but go ye rather to them that sell, and buy for yourselves. And while they went to buy, the bridegroom came; and they that were ready went in with him to the marriage: and the door was shut. Afterward came also the other virgins, saying, Lord, Lord, open to us. But he answered and said, Verily I say unto you, I know you not."

As we read this text we see a clear distinction made between the virgins who are accepted and those who are rejected. The Scripture tells us that one group is wise and the other group is foolish. The Greek word for wise is *phronimos* and means to be mindful of one's interest. The Greek root of this is defined as to reign in or curb the mind. These virgins were wise because they had learned to curb the desire of natural wisdom and had burned with a desire for true wisdom of God. The word for foolish is *mōros* it is defined as godless. Its root defines it as lacking hidden wisdom or the mysteries of God. Whether you know it or not the amount of intimacy you have with God and His wisdom determines the amount of anointing and fire of God in operation in your life. Five of the virgins anticipated the Bridegrooms return and were ready and waiting, but the other five lost intimacy and became dependant on men to give them the anointing and intimacy they desperately needed. The true Bride of Christ will follow the will of God with intimate passion and desire, and they will be granted power and authority to rule and reign with Christ.

I John 2:27

"These *things* have I written unto you concerning them that seduce you. ²⁷But the anointing which ye have received of him abideth in you, and ye need not that any man teach you: but as the same anointing teacheth you of all things, and is truth, and is no lie, and even as it hath taught you, ye shall abide in him."

It is the true desire for personal intimacy, and obedience to God's Word that will determine those who join themselves to the true Bride of Christ. Within the translation of the Song of Solomon you are about to read, you will find a clear description of who the Bride is to the Bridegroom, who the Bridegroom is to the Bride, as well as the attitude and response of the virgins who have not kept their oath and commitment to God. When the Scripture speaks of virgins it is not referencing a gender, but rather a group of individuals who are bound in commitment together. It is God's will that all of the churches join His Bride, but the mindset of each virgin group will either hinder or help the progression. Through this translation you will see a singular virgin followed by the word companions. The word companion denotes the varied individuals who make up the virgin Bride. You will also see the term my dove, this is a term of endearment from the Bridegroom to His Bride. The Bridegroom also refers to His Bride as His sister. This expresses the idea of royalty marrying into the same family to keep the bloodline pure. Some other references that you will find in this translation will be a reference to Tirzah, one of the five virgin daughters of Zelophehad who reclaimed their inheritance in the land of promise. Their father's name means firstborn, representing Jesus being the firstborn among many brethren that gives each of us a right to become His Bride and enter in. To understand the reference of Tirzah you must understand that her name carries with it the name of favorable and pleasant. Another interesting reference is one of David and his warfare of praise, another that of Solomon's palanquin. A palanquin is a chair of royalty carried around by four servants. Each of the ornaments on Solomon's palanquin represent spiritual qualities carried by the Bride, and the servants carrying the chair conveys the plurality of the Bride unified by the spark of love.

As you read this translation of the Song of Solomon for the first time, may you be inspired to go deeper in your walk with Jesus so that you may be a part of the true Bride of Christ destined to rule and reign with Him eternally. After you read it once, reread it over and over. I believe that other references in Scripture will be illuminated as you study the spiritual translation of this book.

Song of Solomon Roles

Song of Solomon — A song written for the Christian who desires completeness, welfare, soundness and safety, as they travel through a world of distraction, chaos, and compromised people.

Bridegroom - Jesus Christ, the Word of God made flesh, the true lover of the church who laid down His life for her perfection.

Virgins — A representation of the multiple church groups and organizations that say they want Jesus, but continue to operate in varied beliefs based on worldly operations, personal opinion, and personal comfort.

Virgin — a representation of the true bride who continues to run after the Truth. A group of saints sanctified by obedience to the Holy Spirit and the

Word, desiring to grow to the full measure of Jesus Christ through His Lordship.

Companions – People who are together as intimate friends, supporters, and partners in a company or fellowship

Watchmen - The leadership of the varied church groups who have been given the responsibility of serving, and protecting God's family on the earth by teaching the full counsel of God and yielding to the works of the Spirit, without compromise for personal agenda, monetary gain, or popularity with men.

My Dove – God's term of endearment to the virgin bride anticipating His coming union.

The Song Of Solomon

Chapter One

The traveler's song of songs, which is completeness, soundness, welfare, peace.

[2] **Virgin:** Let the Bridegroom equip me with the equipping of His Word: for His love *is* better than His wrath. [3] Because of the sweet aroma of His sacrifice, and His beneficial anointing, His name is as anointing oil emptied and poured out, therefore do the virgins love Him. [4] Seize us and draw us, we will run after You: the King has carried us into His innermost parts and

enclosed us: we will tremble, rejoice and be glad in Him, we will keep our minds fixed on our intoxicating love: those on a straight and upright path love You.

[5]**Bridegroom:** I am looking diligently and seeking you, I am coming after a beautiful shepherd and a flock, O ye virgins who say you follow the teaching of peace, but dwell and grow dark, covering the evil and grievous, but still desire safety and peace. [6]Don't look to Me, because I am seeking, and the bright light will see you: those that cause division among my building

will be burned! They made me the keeper of their vineyards; My own vineyard will I guard. [7]Tell me, O virgin who loves and desires the breath of life, who are you associating with and where do you graze? Where do you stretch yourself out and lie down? Whose roof do you go under to obtain the blessing? What, should I cover, envelop, and unite myself to a flock that is lacking and needy? [8]If you do not know where you dwell, O beautiful one among the virgins, exit and leave the heels of the sheep and goats, and let the young goats graze at the true Shepherd's habitation. ⁹Become like your companions, be quick and joyful to operate in a great house, be like a team running together. ¹⁰Be soft and dwell in order, like a stone that is perforated to be bound together on a chain. ¹¹Work to be fashioned into my order, into the brilliance and splendor of the precious metal fixed into a place. This is my desire.

¹²**Virgin:** When the King comes to inspect my surroundings, I will be like light, giving him sacrifices that are genuine and pure, like the sweet aroma of spikenard. ¹³Like myrrh

in a bundle, I will be bound together in His strength, boiling with love, abiding with Him in the night, taking His Lordship into my bosom [14] My Beloved is a lover who ransoms, a spring of sacrifice, paying the price of life for His vineyard [15] Behold, He is bright and handsome to His virgin, fair and beautiful, flowing like a spring of wine, deep in color like the eyes of the dove. [16] Behold, He is handsome, my Beloved, like the sweet song from a singer, pleasant and generous to anyone: His bed *is* luxurious, fresh, and flourishing. [17] His house within is established, purified, and made firm, a turned work of stateliness.

Chapter 2

Bridegroom: I am the rose of the upright, making all things straight, exalting the unsearchable depths of the valleys, ²displaying joy in the piercing, an intimate companion to my virgin. ³I breathe sweet words of life that flow to make firm, I am intoxicating love among my children. Sit down and abide under the shadow of my protection, desire to bear fruit. Become sweet, pleasing, and dedicated.

⁴**Virgin:** He brought me to His intoxicating house to be built up,

and I beheld His standard of love. [5]I said, let me lean upon your foundation, revive me with your wine, and refresh me with your breath: for I am weak for Your love. [6]He wrapped me up and covered my whole left side, and His right hand embraced me. [7]I adjure you to take an oath, virgins who believe the teaching of peace, whether you are a roe, glorious and prominent, or a hind, spread across another field, open your eyes, and wake up, so my love will be pleased. [8]I hear the voice of my Beloved calling!

Bridegroom: "Come in to the mountain of God leaping, be gathered to the hill of Zion."

[9]**Virgin**: My Beloved wants you to be like Him, full of splendor and glory like the roe, strong in leadership like the young hart: He looks to see who will take a stand behind Him, He longs to see who will shine and sparkle, and catches them in His net. [10]My Beloved speaks and says

Bridegroom: "Arise, become powerful and be fixed, my excellent virgin and companions, walk with me. [11]Hide no more, the storm is passed over, the violent rain has changed and departed. ¹²The blossoms appear on the earth; an occasion has come for us to touch and sing the songs of praise. I am calling to hear the voice of my dove within the earth. ¹³The fig tree is producing ripe fruit, and the noble vine is blossoming giving the smell of sacrifice. Arise, become powerful and be fixed, my excellent virgin and companions, walk with me.¹⁴My dove, that has taken refuge and been concealed in the Rock, in the secret hidden place ascending the steps of the mountain, let Me look upon you and inspect My vision, let Me hear your voice; your voice gives Me pleasure, and your appearing is beautiful. [15]Take hold of the foxes, the insignificant foxes, that bind and corrupt the noble vine: for the noble vine is blossoming."

[16]**Virgin:** My beloved is a shepherd, a ruler, a teacher, a companion, and friend who feeds His people with great exaltation and joy. [17]Until that day comes, and the heat departs, and the darkness flees, resemble Him by becoming full of splendor and glory like the roe, strong in leadership like the young

hart separating your self into the cleft of the mountain of God.

Chapter 3

Virgin: [1]At midnight I laid down for His intimacy; I desired to be refreshed by my love, I searched for His encounter. [2]I stood up, turned in excitement, and ran to find Him in the streets and open places. I sought the breath of life, which I love. I searched to find what was lost. [3]The watchmen that go around the city found me: I said, "Have you seen the One I long after, the One with the breath of life?" [4]In a few moments, I ceased to exist and passed over to find Him, the breath of life I love. I seized

Him by the hand and yielded to relaxed abandonment. I said "Come lets depart and be intimate within the inner chamber so I can conceive."[5] I adjure you to take an oath, virgins who believe the teaching of peace, whether you are a roe, glorious and prominent, or a hind, spread across another field, open your eyes, and wake up, so my love will be pleased.

[6] The time has come to ascend out of the uninhabited wilderness; like the pillar of smoke that rises, or the sun that climbs the sky. Let us stand strong and upright like the

palm, by making a sacrifice of brokenness, a sacrifice of grieving, holy and white, crushed to powder, purchased with price.

[7] Stretch out on His bed, it is a place of completeness, soundness, welfare, and peace. Let men become strong, mighty, and powerful as they assemble round about it, and wrestle with Him until God prevails. [8] Seize the two edged-sword, learn and be trained to fight. Let men exist, and take a stand with the sword upon their loins, because there is terror in the night. [9] Become a king and reign in

completeness and peace, like productive Solomon who was carried upon a palanquin of pure white. [10]He fashioned it by taking a stand, longing for the pure and precious metal of wisdom, supported by the brilliance and splendor of the golden oil, carried within in the upright and virtuous color of purple, riding in the middle among servants fit together sparked with love. Hear me virgins following the teaching of peace, [11]come forth. See your King of peace, crowned, dividing and departing, giving out crowns in the hot day of His marriage, in the day of His joyful banquets of the inner man of the heart.

Chapter 4

Bridegroom: Behold, you are beautiful and excellent, My fair companions. You are good and pleasant, My dove. Your eyes are like fountains springing forth from behind your veil. Your hair is set in order like a secure army of witnesses in battle array, appearing in the Mount of God. ²The teeth of My flock, is teaching, words like a sharp weapon that pierce and cut off, ivory coming out of a washing, joined together, without one being barren. ³From behind your veil your lips bring forth speech sown together like a thread of crimson, saying befitting words of abode. Your cheeks bring forth many pieces that form a single fruit resembling the pomegranate [4]Your neck is growing, straight and narrow, becoming great in power and praise like David the beloved, a established arsenal of weapons, a family of ten thousand defenders lifting up their shields, mastering power and dominion. [5]I repeatedly return to you, like a child partaking from the breast, watching as you violently destroy and pulverize your enemy in battle, when we become joined together, we feed on the song of rejoicing. [6:17]Until that day comes, and the heat departs, and the darkness flees, I will come into the mount of God and flow like oil, and I will ascend the hill of holy purified worship. [7]You are beautiful and good, My love; without spot and blemish.

[8]Come with Me to be white, My Bride, Come with Me to be white: Join with Me, your supreme head and high Prince, See our covenant of faith, point yourself to the mountain of snow , be devoted to the sanctuary, plucked from the

violent lions, and the lair of jackals, come to the mountain of the pure. ⁹You have ravished My heart, My sister, My Bride; you have ravished My heart and My eyes are fixed to unite with you, you are My slave of love and I will adorn you with gifts ¹⁰How beautiful and pleasant is your love, My sister, My Bride! It's so pleasant it's boiling and intoxicating! I breathe in the odor of your sacrifice; it is a very fruitful anointing, smelling better to Me than any other fragrance! ¹¹Your Speech, O Bride, is like a discourse of preaching or prophecy dripping like the honeycomb, the sweet and most excellent words flow from your tongue. I accept and delight in the garments covering your figure; I accept it in its whiteness. [12]I will enclose you in the Garden of Eden, and fasten the door with a bolt, My sister, My Bride; you will be a spring shut up, a fountain sealed. [13]You will sprout and let loose a enclosed garden, rising up like the fruit of the pomegranates, eminent fruitfulness, ransomed with the price of life, a genuine and pure dedication [14]Genuine light and costly gold; bought and erected, firm, holy, and white; a flowing fragrant honeymoon suite, with all the fragrances of the high Prince: ¹⁵fountains in a enclosed garden, wells of living waters, and streams purified.

Virgin: Wake up, hidden ones, and go in at His right side, pant for His garden, so the fragrance may pour down. Let My Beloved come into His garden, and eat His pleasant fruit.

Chapter 5

Bridegroom: ¹Come in, to My enclosed garden. I have gathered and reaped My harvest, plucking My grapes from My vine. They flow together like oil releasing its fragrance. With vigor, I long to partake of the sweet, Let's drink at this intoxicating banquet and grow to a place of wealth and abundance. Eat, My intimate friends, drink, and drink to the full, My beloved.

Virgin: ²I was sleeping, but my inner man was stirred, My Beloved called aloud and beat violently upon my door, he said

Bridegroom: "Open up, be freed and loosed, My sister, My companions, My dove, for you are undefiled, complete, and pure. Your head Prince is long full of the mist of the night, having been cut, wounded, broken, and ruined by it's gloom."

Virgin: I said [3] I have already taken off my robe, how shall I be recovered? My feet are clean, do you want them to get soiled?" [4]My Beloved, dismissed me and let go of the hole in the door, and my inner parts were troubled with great uproar and commotion. ⁵I rose up and longed to be freed and loosed by my Beloved; and my hands grasped and reached out to flow with Him in sweet fragrance, I bowed myself down and touched my hand upon the bolt. ⁶I opened to my Beloved; but my Beloved had withdrawn himself, and was gone: my very soul failed, I could not speak: I sought to find Him; I cried out to Him, but heard no answer. ⁷The shepherds, keepers, and watchmen that went about the city found me, they smote me, they bruised me; the keepers of the walls took away my veil. [8]I Said "I adjure you to take an oath, O virgins of the teaching of peace, if you find my beloved, tell him, that I am weak for His love.

Virgins: [9]What is so special about your beloved that you would desire to be His wife? Why do you love Him so, that you ask in such a manner for us to take an oath?

Virgin: [10]My Beloved is dazzling, bright, white, clear, wearing garments stained with blood. He is a standard that covers millions [11]He is the Head that has come to shake man, family, city, nation, and the priests, hiding the stains, but bringing forth purified gold. He was cut and wounded, but exalted and lofty, passionately seeking to end the darkness like the setting sun. [12]He sees and longs for the deep fountain waters of His dove, desiring to wash her with abundance, and abiding fullness. [13]His cheek is soft, a place to ascend to, and a fragrant tower where the anointing oil is prepared: His speech flows with dripping prophecy that impregnates and carries great joy. [14]His hands are full of strength and power, shimmering with precious metal and precious stones, rolling and turning, breaking and subjecting them until they are complete. His heart's desire is to teach us to be formable, taking count of each stone as he covers it. [15]His legs run after us to make us white, an ordained, established, and ruling foundation of purity. He sees a vision of pure white, choosing and selecting those who are firm and stable. [16]His mouth desires to taste the dedicated and sweet: that is the object of His desire. This *is* my Beloved, and this *is* my Friend, O virgins of the teaching of peace.

Chapter 6

Virgins: Where has your beloved gone, O beautiful bride? Why has He turned away from you? Answer our request.

Virgin: ²My beloved is gone down to defend and surround His enclosed garden, to the flower beds where the plants are trained in sweet fragrance, to tend to the plants in the garden, and to gather up those who are white and exalted with joy. ³I am my Beloved's, and my Beloved *is* mine: He rules and teaches His flock to be glad and rejoicing.

Bridegroom: [4]You are excellent, good, and beautiful, O My love, like Tirzah, one of the daughters of Zelophehad of Manassah who was favorably accepted, a befitting flock following the teaching of peace, to be feared like a army holding the banner of My standard. [5]These encircle Me and fix their eyes upon Me, they press and urge Me: My flocks commitment causes disarray, they are strong, robust, and powerful, sitting down on the hill of witness. [6]The teeth of my flock, is teaching, words like a sharp weapon that pierces and cuts off, ivory coming out of a washing, joined together, without one being barren. [7]Your cheeks bring forth many pieces that form a single fruit resembling the pomegranate,[8] made up of a increasing number of men growing into royalty, a group of plenteous married lovers, virgins innumerable. [9]My dove is perfect and completely one; one nation or metropolis, a great and leading city. She is tested and proven, pure, clean and sincere. She is one who brings forth. The virgins look upon her and she is straight and right, a bride of royalty, married to her lover, God's shining light. [10]Who *is* my bride? She looks down upon the earth from God's Mountain, breaking forth like the dawn, beautiful, shining white like the reflecting moon in the night, as pure as the heat of the sun, a formidable army holding the banner of My standard.

[11]I will descend to My enclosed garden and see if it is fresh and tender towards Me, My possession that produces a river, a planting that bends and breaks forth, like multiple pieces of the pomegranate

lifted up high, and flourishing. [12]I know that My breath of life has been fixed to carry My willing people. [13]Return, return to Me, you perfected bride abiding in the teaching of peace; return, return to Me, that I may look upon you like a prophet in a ecstatic state. I will see the completion of My covenant of peace, and I will dance, and sing in the company of My people.

Chapter 7

Bridegroom: Adorn your feet with shoes that march to My beat, My willing daughter! Be willing to curve at my flank and be adorned with my chain, a undertaking fashioned by God's hands, the Master artisan. ²Let us be connected like a twisting round umbilical cord, or a minstrels string that needs to be struck, without mingling water with wine. Let your womb be hungry to gather in the harvest of wheat, a hedge of song displaying joy. ³I repeatedly return to you, like a child partaking from the breast, watching as you violently destroy and pulverize your enemy in battle. [4]Your neck is growing sharper in teaching, straight and strong; a fountain where men kneel and drink taking in reason and understanding, a way of entrance for My daughter among multitudes. Your anger grows high to see purity as you look closely into the faces of the silent workers. [5]You shake the fruit of the gardens to see if it is choice, or poor and languishing lacking virtue; the choice is placed in the watering trough as royalty. [6]You are adorned with bright beauty, pleasant and delightful, O Love, My delicate desire! ⁷My lover brings forth clusters of fruit. You rise to My stature, standing erect and resembling Me in power and strength, ready to lay waste. ⁸I Say, I will cause you to climb and ascend in your stand, I will seize you by the boughs, I will possess the cluster of your prosperity, I will accept your aroma of sacrifice, as one who breathes intensely, breathing out my life for the fruit. I will taste of your intoxicating pleasant dedication, and I will make your walk straight and even. I will speak out to those who are sleeping, creeping slowly in their slander towards death.

Virgin: [10]I am my Beloved's overflowing desire! [11]Come, my Beloved, let us go forth into the harvest field; let us pass the night beneath Your covering atonement. [12]Let us go up early into this garden; let us look to see if the vines are green, prosperous, and budding. I want to see the blossoming fruit appear, and the pieces within the single pomegranate exalted, lifted up, and shining: there I will give it all to You, My Beloved! [13]I am a basket of sweet smelling sacrifice given to God, offering up my most valuable and precious fruit, both fresh and stored up, a hidden treasure laid up specifically for You!

Chapter 8

Virgins: ¹We want to be given to You to bear your family resemblance, let us taste the sweet intimacy! If we find You outside our door, we will let You kiss us; we will not despise You. ²We will lead you and bring you into our intimate relationship, to instruct You. We will give you a drink of mixed wine from our pomegranate ³⁶Then You should wrap us up and cover our whole left side, and let Your right hand embrace us.

Virgin: ⁴I adjure you to take an oath, virgins who believe the teaching of peace, open your eyes, and wake up, so my love will be pleased.

Bridegroom: ⁵Who *is* this using words to climb up and ascend from a sterile and sandy country, trying to get support and lean on My love? Open your eyes and wake up, you valued My breath very little, you are a nation brought to ruin and spoiled. You were brought forth broken and wicked. ⁶Set the seal of My signet ring upon your inner man, be sealed with My helper: for

God's love is strong breaking death; but a severe jealousy can lead you into hell: a burning heat, burning, *a most vehement flame.* ⁷I have overcome many dangers for you to now quench God's love, allow My stream to inundate you. Whosoever will give all of the wealth and riches of his inward house for God's love will not be despised or insignificant.

Virgins: ⁸We have an insignificant sister, and she has no power. What shall we do for our sister in the hot day of Your speaking? ⁹If she is joined to You, we will make her the necklace of jewels that You long for: and if she is a easily accessible woman, we will enclose her with the stability of your tablets.

Virgin: [10]I am a maiden chaste and difficult to approach joined to Him, I am strong and powerful, laying waste, growing in greatness: I am a spring that hast caught His eye as one that finds completeness, soundness, welfare, and peace.

Bridegroom: [11]Completeness, soundness, welfare, and peace abide in my noble vineyard. I am the Lord possessor of its abundance; I lent out my vineyard to the watchmen, shepherds, and keepers. Every servant was to bring me the purified fruitful family, I longed for, worth its weight in precious metal. [12]My noble vineyard faces me, and is before me without turning. Those who dwell in completeness, soundness, welfare, and peace, are a company under one leader, guarding the fruit of their actions a hundred times. [13]You who dwell in My enclosed garden, unite and be joined together, hear my voice calling, listen and obey!

Virgin. ⁱ⁴Hasten, My Beloved wants you to be like Him, full of splendor and glory like the roe, strong in leadership like the young hart, bringing your sweet aroma to the Mountain of God.

Reference List

Strong's Exhaustive Concordance of the Bible. James Strong. Nashville: Thomas Nelson Publishers, 1984.

Blue Letter Bible. 1996-2012, August 1,2012. <u>www.blueletterbible.org</u>

Gesenius's Lexicon of the Old Testament. S.P. Tragelle. London: Samuel Baxter & Sons, 1857.

For Booking, Products, Ministry Affiliation, or Church Planting go to www. ferventfire.com

To attend a service with us in Tulsa, OK.

Go to www. realchurchministries.com

To be trained for full time ministry

Go to **www.aimministryinstitute.org**

To become a ministry partner register

online at ferventfire.com or write us at:

Fervent Fire Ministries

315 S. Sheridan Road,

Tulsa, OK 74112

All Love Gifts Appreciated!